Snakes are reptiles. They or legs. There are about three thousand different sorts of snakes. Some snakes are very long and some are quite short.

A snake has scales to protect its skin from the hot sun. A snake's skin feels cool and smooth.

As a snake gets bigger, it has to shed its skin. The skin looks dull when it is about to be shed. The snake rubs its nose to loosen the old skin, which splits to let the snake slide out.

Snakes can glide on the ground and slide up trees. As a snake slithers along, the scales on the underside of its body grip onto the ground. Some snakes can swim too.

Snakes need the sun, but they cannot cool down by themselves. They have to hide from very hot sun. When it is cool, snakes are sluggish and sleepy.

Snakes normally hatch from eggs. The eggs have strong, leathery shells which do not crack if they are dropped.

A snake hides its eggs in holes in the ground or sand, or in gaps in rocks. A young snake is born with an egg tooth to help it get out of the egg when it hatches.

An adder has zigzag markings on its back. It is poisonous but the poison cannot kill you. An adder's eggs hatch inside its body so the young adders are born alive.

Some snakes spend the whole winter sleeping. They look for a hole to shelter inside, in the ground, or in a rock or a tree. They do not wake up again until spring comes.

Snakes are hunters. The bones in a snake's mouth are joined together quite loosely so they can spread wide apart to fit food in. The skin stretches around the food, too, as if it were made of elastic.

Rattlesnakes, or rattlers, live in North America. A rattler has a bit of dead scale at the tip of its tail. When it shakes its tail, the dead scale makes a buzzing, rattling sound.

rattler

Rattlers hunt small animals such as frogs, toads, and lizards. But rattlers are hunted themselves, too, by king snakes, opossums, and roadrunners.

The biggest sorts of snakes are called constrictors. When it catches an animal, a constrictor coils its body around the animal and squeezes it hard.

The anaconda, which lives in South America, is the biggest snake of all. Anacondas can be more than 30 feet long.

Some snakes are poisonous and have poison, called venom. When a snake bites, it injects venom into its victim with its fangs.

The poison can be milked from the snakes. It can be used to make an antidote so that if a snake bites someone, they can be made better.